# Bridge Game Summary

## *Easy Reference & Game Companion*

## By Samir Riad

**Layout by Amy Sirota**

Copyright ©2009 by Samir Riad
**ISBN:1-4392-4042-6**
- All Rights Reserved -
www.BridgeGameSummary.com

To order additional copies, please contact
BookSurge Publishing
1-866-308-6235

**Available online at
www.amazon.com**

# BRIDGE GAME SUMMARY

♣   ♥

## Table of Contents

# BRIDGE GAME SUMMARY

♣    ♥

# INTRODUCTION

**Bridge Game Summary**
*Easy Reference & Game*
*Companion*

I wrote **Bridge Game Summary** to be a game table companion for all Bridge players. All games have a brief instruction manual included in the game box to help the players learn how to play. Why not do the same for Bridge? That's why I wrote this book.

In this book, I explain the idea of the Bridge game and how to start playing in a brief and easy to understand way. I include color reference tables for bidding and playing the hand. Most of the more popular Bridge conventions have been included, although you don't really need many of them to win and enjoy the game. I also felt it important to include scoring reference tables and instructions on how to keep score. The requirements for bidding and playing a game have been updated according to the most current guidelines.

Bridge Game Summary combines the easy reference of color tables with a brief explanation of how to play the game. It's the best of both worlds for beginners and casual Bridge players alike.

# BRIDGE GAME SUMMARY

♣    ♥

# GETTING STARTED

## The Object of The Game

1. You need four players to play Bridge.

2. Each two players that sit opposite each other are partners.

3. Each time the cards are distributed, it's a new "hand" and one team plays offense and the other team plays defense.

4. The way to determine who plays which position is by "bidding".

5. Each team after looking at their cards bid to win a certain number of tricks. A trick is a round of cards where each player played a card.

6. The team that bids the highest, wins the bidding, plays offense, and has a chance to score a *game*.

7. The team that bids the lowest, loses the bidding, plays defense, and can still score points if they can prevent the other team from making their bid.

8. When one team scores two games, that is called a "rubber. That's a Bridge term that means a partial match like a set in the game of tennis.

9. Bonus points are awarded to the team that scores games and rubbers.

10. A friendly Bridge game is usually more than one rubber and can be as many rubbers as the players agree to play.

11. At the end, the team with the most points wins the game.

## The Four Stages of Bridge

| Stage | Description | Details |
|---|---|---|
| 1 | **Starting the Game**<br><br>Picking Partners, shuffling and dealing the cards. | The game requires 4 players, each two players that sit across each other are partners. The dealer distributes the cards to each player one card at a time until all the cards are dealt – 13 cards each. |
| 2 | **Bidding**<br><br>• Opening bid.<br>• Responding bid.<br>• Overcall bid.<br>• Bidding for a game.<br>• Bidding for a slam. | Each player organizes the cards in his hand by suits. Next, you count the value of your cards. The dealer starts the bidding stage, and every player either bid higher or passes. When 3 players pass in a row, the bidding stage ends. A trump suit (special suit) will be picked for playing the hand, and sometimes no trump is picked. The bid winner who will play the hand is called the Declarer. |
| 3 | **Playing the Hand**<br><br>• The opening lead.<br>• Opening the dummy's hand.<br>• Playing offense.<br>• Playing defense. | Playing the hand stage starts by the opening lead. This is the first card played and always played by the player on the left of the Declarer. After the opening lead, the Declarer's partner becomes the Dummy. He opens his cards, put them on the table face up, and does not participate in playing the hand.<br><br>The Declarer will play both his hand and his partner's hand. This gives the Declarer total control over playing the hand. The opening lead could be in any suit and all other players must follow the suit. The highest card wins the trick. The winner of each trick plays again and the play continues until all the cards are played and the hand is completed. |
| 4 | **Keeping the score**<br><br>• Scoring game points.<br>• Down points.<br>• Rubber and slams points.<br>• Bonus points. | After all the tricks are played, the scoring stage begins. Each team counts their winning tricks and a designated player writes down the score. Points will be awarded for scoring partial games and games. Bonuses will be awarded for scoring a Rubber (a set of two games) and bonuses will be awarded for winning all the tricks in the hand ( Grand Slam), or winning all the tricks except one (Small Slam). Also points will be awarded to the opposite team for preventing their opponents from making their bid. Bonus points will be awarded for having the four aces, for having 4 or 5 honors in one suit, or scoring extra tricks. The team with the most points wins the game. |

## Getting started:

1.  The deck of cards has 52 cards.

2.  There are four suits in the deck: Spades (♠), Hearts (♥), Diamonds (♦), and Clubs (♣). They rank in that order where Spades is the highest rank and Clubs is the lowest rank.

3.  Each suit consists of 13 cards. The four high cards, Ace (A), King (K), Queen (Q), and Jack (J) are also called the 4 honors. Then 10, 9, 8, 7, 6, 5, 4, 3, and 2. The rank is in this order, where the Ace is the highest and the 2 is the lowest.

4.  It takes four players to play Bridge. Each two players sitting across from each other are partners, and they add up their tricks together. North and South are partners. West and East are partners.

```
      North

West        East

      South
```

Each player draws a card from the deck. The two highest cards partner together and the two lowest cards partner together. The player with the highest card deals, chooses the deck of cards, and chooses where to sit.

The dealer (D) distributes the cards to each player one card at a time starting from the left. You deal clockwise around the table until all the cards are dealt. Now each player has 13 cards.

Each player should organize his cards in suits. Starting with the Spades on the left, then Hearts, Clubs, and Diamonds. The suits are also organized in alternate colors (black, red, black, and red). It's easier to see the cards this way.

## Organizing Your Hand in Suits and Colors:

## Counting the Value of your Cards

In order to determine the strength of your hand, you need to count your points. The four honors (high cards) have a point value. The Jack is 1 point, the Queen is 2 points, the King is 3 points, and the Ace is 4 points.

In addition to the Honor points, there are also distribution points. If you don't have a card in any suit (Void), that's 3 points. If you have only one card in any suit (Singleton), that's 2 points. If you have only two cards in any suit (Doubleton) that's 1 point.

If you have the four honors in any suit, that equals 10 points. Since there are four suits in the deck of cards, the total honor points in the game are 40.

| Honors | Points | Distribution* | Points |
|---|---|---|---|
| Ace (A) | 4 points | Void | 3 points |
| King (K) | 3 points | Singleton | 2 points |
| Queen (Q) | 2 points | Doubleton | 1 points |
| Jack (J) | 1 points | *Not used in No Trump bids. | |

## The Four Suits

The four suits (or the four trumps) in the deck of cards in the order of their value are:

- ♣ Clubs – Trick value 20 points
- ♦ Diamonds – Trick value 20 points
- ♥ Hearts – Trick value 30 points
- ♠ Spades – Trick value 30 points

Clubs are the lowest value and rank. Spades are the highest value and rank.

## No Trump "NT"

No trump "NT" is playing without a designated trump (suit). The trick value of NT is 40 points for the first trick and 30 points for each additional trick after that. NT is the highest value and the highest rank in Bridge.

♠ ♦

# BRIDGE GAME SUMMARY

## Winning the Trick

A trick is a round of four cards where each player played one card. Each time the cards are dealt, it's a new hand with 13 tricks to play. Once a card is led in any suit, the other players must play the same suit as long as they have it. You win the trick if you play the highest card in the led suit.

When playing with a designated trump and out of the led suit, you can also win the trick by playing a trump card. It's like playing a wild card – it beats any other card in the deck except for a higher trump.

## Trick Values

| Suit | Trick Value |
|---|---|
| No Trump | 40 points* |
| Spade | 30 points |
| Heart | 30 points |
| Diamond | 20 points |
| Club | 20 points |

* For the 1st trick, then 30 for each following trick.

## What is "Book"?

Since the total number of tricks in each hand is 13 tricks, then in order for your partnership to win the hand, you should win the majority of the 13 tricks, which is 7 tricks or more. The winner always wins more than 6 tricks, so in Bridge we call the first 6 tricks won by the Declarer "book" and we count the winning tricks (1-7) over book.

We use the 1-7 tricks when we bid, play the hand or write the score, with the understanding that "book" is added to it. You score 1 when you win 1 trick over book. You score 2 when you win 2 tricks over book and so on.

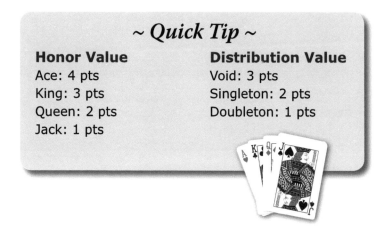

### ~ *Quick Tip* ~

**Honor Value**
Ace: 4 pts
King: 3 pts
Queen: 2 pts
Jack: 1 pts

**Distribution Value**
Void: 3 pts
Singleton: 2 pts
Doubleton: 1 pts

# BRIDGE GAME SUMMARY

# BIDDING

1. To open bidding is to bid in one of the four suits (also called trumps). The player can also choose to open in no designated suit, which is called "no trump".

2. The bidding always progresses by going up like an auction. When a player opens, the next player must bid higher. You can't win an auction by bidding lower – you always go higher.

3. Bidding goes up both in rank of the suits and in levels. The four suits rank in alphabetical order from the lowest to the highest: Clubs, Diamonds, Hearts, and Spades. "No Trump" ranks higher than Spades and is the highest "suit" bid in the game.

4. The levels are numbered "one", "two", "three", etc. The first level is the "one" level; 1 Club, 1 Diamond, 1 Heart, 1 Spade, and 1 No Trump from lowest to highest in that order. The "two" level is: 2 Clubs, 2 Diamonds, 2 Hearts, 2 Spades, and 2 No Trumps, in that order. You go up the levels and the suit ranks until "7 No Trump" which is the highest bid possible in the game.

| Level One | 1 ♣ | **Opening points** | **The Bidding Levels** |
|---|---|---|---|
| | 1 ♦ | Minimum hand:13-15 pts | |
| | 1 ♥ | Medium hand:16-18 pts | |
| | 1 ♠ | Maximum hand:19-21 pts | |
| | 1 NT | 15-17 Honor pts | |
| Level Two | 2 ♣ | **Opening points** | **Honor points:** |
| | 2 ♦ | 21-25 pts | Ace (4), King (3), Queen (2), and Jack (1). |
| | 2 ♥ | | |
| | 2 ♠ | | |
| | 2 NT | 20-21 Honor pts | |
| Level Three | 3 ♣ | **Opening points** | **Distribution Points:** |
| | 3 ♦ | 6-10 pts | Void (3), Singleton (2), and Doubleton (1). |
| | 3 ♥ | (Pre-emptive bid) | |
| | 3 ♠ | | |
| | 3 NT | Game: 25 Honor pts | |
| Level Four | 4 ♣ | **Game** | |
| | 4 ♦ | 4 ♥ or 4 ♠ | |
| | 4 ♥ | 25 Team pts | In no trumps, count your honor points only. In all other bids, count both your honor and distribution points. |
| | 3 ♠ | | |
| | 4 NT | | |
| Level Five | 5 ♣ | **Game** | |
| | 5 ♦ | 5 ♣ or 5 ♦ | |
| | 5 ♥ | 29 Team pts | |
| | 4 ♠ | | |
| | 5 NT | | |
| Level Six | 6 ♣ | **Small Slam** | |
| | 6 ♦ | 33 Team pts | |
| | 6 ♥ | | |
| | 6 ♠ | | |
| | 6 NT | Requires: 33 Honor pts | |
| Level Seven | 7 ♣ | **Grand Slam** | |
| | 7 ♦ | 37 Team pts | |
| | 7 ♥ | | |
| | 7 ♠ | | |
| | 7 NT | Requires: 37 Honor pts | |

♣ ♥

## Opening 1 in a Suit:

You need 13-21 points (total honor and distribution points) and a 5-card suit or more to open 1 in a suit. If you have 13-15 points, it is considered a low opening, while 19-21 points is a high opening.

Each player picks his best suit to open with. It could be Spades, Hearts, Diamonds or Clubs – any suit is fine. Your best suit is the longest suit (the suit with the most cards). The minimum requirement in the opening suit is 5 cards and at least 2-3 honors.

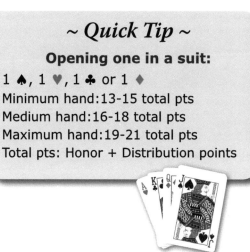

*~ Quick Tip ~*

**Opening one in a suit:**

1 ♠, 1 ♥, 1 ♣ or 1 ♦
Minimum hand:13-15 total pts
Medium hand:16-18 total pts
Maximum hand:19-21 total pts
Total pts: Honor + Distribution points

# BRIDGE GAME SUMMARY

Below are some practice hands showing 1 suit openings:

Honor points: 16
Distribution points: 1
5 cards in Spades

## Bid: 1 Spade

Honor points: 18
Distribution points: 1
5 cards in Hearts

## Bid: 1 Heart

Honor points: 15
Distribution points: 1
5 cards in Clubs

## Bid: 1 Club

Honor points: 17
Distribution points: 1
5 cards in Diamonds

## Bid: 1 Diamond

Honor points: 15
Distribution points: 3
5 cards in Spades

## Bid: 1 Spade

Honor points: 12
Distribution points: 1
5 cards in Hearts

## Bid: 1 Heart

Honor points: 12
Distribution points: 1
5 cards in Clubs

## Bid: 1 Club

Honor points: 12
Distribution points: 2
5 cards in Diamonds

## Bid: 1 Diamond

## Opening 2, in a Suit:

To open 2 in a suit you must have 21-25 points, and 5-7 cards in that suit. Below are some practice hands showing 2 suit's opening.

♠ A K Q J 5 3
♥ A K
♣ K Q 7
♦ 10 4

Honor points: 22
Distribution points: 2
6 cards in Spades

Bid: 2 Spades

♠ A K 10 9
♥ A K Q 9 5
♣ A Q 5 2
♦

Honor points: 22
Distribution points: 3
5 cards in Hearts

Bid: 2 Hearts

♠ 5
♥ A K 5
♣ A K Q J 8 7
♦ K J 10

Honor points: 21
Distribution points: 2
6 cards in Clubs

Bid: 2 Clubs

♠ K 9
♥ A K 5
♣ Q 2
♦ A K Q J 10 4

Honor points: 22
Distribution points: 2
6 cards in Diamonds

Bid: 2 Diamonds

### ~ Quick Tip ~

#### Opening Two in a Suit

If your partner opens 2 of a suit it is called a "demand bid". You can't respond with a pass to a 2 opening bid even with 0 points. The reason is that your partner has so many points that, in most cases he can make more than two on his own. You should keep the bidding going until a game is reached.

♠  ♦

## Opening 3, in a Suit:

Opening 3 in a suit requires 6-10 honor points and a long suit of 7 cards or longer. The reason that you can bid so high with so few honor points is that you can anticipate that most of your trump cards, even your low ones, will win tricks because you have so many of them.

Below are some practice hands showing 3 suit openings.

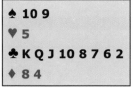

Honor points: 6
Distribution points: 4
8 cards in Clubs
Bid: 3 Clubs

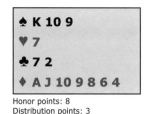

Honor points: 8
Distribution points: 3
7 cards in Diamonds
Bid: 3 Diamonds

## Opening in No Trump:

If the bidder doesn't have a 5-card opening suit, but has at least 15-17 points (all honor points), balanced distribution (no void, no singleton), and 3 suits protected by high honors, he can open 1 No Trump*.

In order to open 2 No Trump, you need 20-21 points, with all 4 suits protected by high honors.

*Playing without designated trump suit.*

To open 3 No Trump, you should have 25-27 points and all suits protected as well.

♠ K Q 9 3
♥ K J 8
♣ 10 4 2
♦ A Q 10

Honor points: 15
Distribution points: 0
Balanced distribution

Bid: 1 No Trump

♠ K Q 9
♥ A Q 10 9
♣ A Q 2
♦ A 10 4

Honor points: 21
Distribution points: 0
Balanced distribution

Bid: 2 No Trump

♠ A K 9 3
♥ A K J 9
♣ A Q 2
♦ A 4

Honor points: 25
Distribution points: 0
Balanced distribution

Bid: 3 No Trump

**BIDDING**

## ~ *Quick Tips* ~

### Opening 1 NT

**Points:** 15-17 Honor points

**Balanced Distribution:** No void, no singleton. (Cards break by suit: 4-3-3-3, or 4-4-3-2, or 5-3-3-2)

**3 suits protected:** one or more winners in each of the 3 suits.

# The table below will summarize the proper opening bids depending on the strength in your hand.

## Table 1: Opening Bids

| Opening | Points | Suit | Comments |
|---|---|---|---|
| **1 suit** (Minimum hand) | 13-15 | 5-card suit | Choose a major suit over a minor suit. If you have two equal suits, bid the higher ranking one first. |
| **1 suit** (Medium hand) | 16-18 | | |
| **1 suit** (Maximum hand) | 19-21 | | |
| **2 suit** (Demand bid) | 21-25 | 5-7 card suit | Opening two is a demand bid. Your partner must not say "pass" until a game is reached. |
| **3 suit** (Pre-emptive) | 6-10 Honor Points | 7 card suit or longer | Count your quick tricks, and add 2 if vulnerable, or add 3 when not vulnerable. |
| **1 No Trump** | 15-17 Honor Points | No void, no singleton. Three suits protected. | Balanced distribution, suits break 4-3-3-3, or 4-4-3-2, or 5-3-3-2 |
| **2 No Trump** | 20-21 Honor Points | No void, no singleton. Four suits protected. | Balanced distribution |
| **3 No Trump** | 25-27 Honor Points | No void, no singleton. Four suits protected. | Balanced distribution |

## Responding to 1, in a suit:

Responding to a one suit opener is the most common response in Bridge. If you have less than 6 points you should pass. If you have opening hand and 12+ points you should jump up a level to signal your strength to your partner.

Below are the three options that you have when you respond to a 1 suit opening.

**Option 1:** If you have a minimum hand of 6-9 points and 3 trump cards in the opening suit, respond 2 in the opening suit. If the opening bid was 1 ♥, your response bid should be 2 ♥. The reason behind this bid is the trump count. It's understood that your partner opened with 5 trumps. If you have 3, then your total trump count is 8, which is enough to play the hand in this trump suit if you wish. With 12+ points you should jump a level and respond 3 ♥.

### ~ Quick Tip ~

**Responding Bid**

Minimum hand: 6-9 points
Medium hand: 10-11 points
Maximum hand: 12+ points

**Option 2:** Your second option is to bid a suit of your own. In that case you need 7-10 points and at least 4 cards in that suit headed by two honors. With 12+ points you should jump a level.

**Option 3:** If you can't respond in the opening suit and you don't have a suit of your own, you bid 1 No Trump. Your partner will understand that you have at least a minimum hand but no 3 cards in the opening suit, and no strong 4-card suit of your own.

## Examples of responding bids to 1 suit opening:

| Option 1: | Option 2: | Option 3: |
|---|---|---|
| **Opening Bid**<br>1 ♥ | **Opening Bid**<br>1 ♣ | **Opening Bid**<br>1 ♥ |
| **Your hand:** | **Your hand** | **Your hand** |
| ♠ A 9 3 | ♠ A K 10 8 | ♠ A K 5 |
| ♥ Q 9 5 | ♥ J 10 8 7 | ♥ 10 7 |
| ♣ K 6 2 | ♣ 9 7 | ♣ 9 8 7 2 |
| ♦ 10 8 5 2 | ♦ Q 10 4 | ♦ J 10 4 2 |
| 9 points<br>Support in Hearts<br>No biddable suit | 11 points<br>Not enough Clubs<br>Biddable Spade suit | 9 points<br>Not enough Hearts<br>No biddable suit |
| **Your response**<br>2 ♥ | **Your response**<br>1 ♠ | **Your response**<br>1 No Trump |

♣    ♥

## Responding to an opening 2 bid in a suit:

If your partner opens 2 in a suit it is called a "demand bid". You can't respond with a pass to a 2 opening bid even with 0 points. The reason is that your partner has so many points (21-25 points) that, in most cases, he can make more than two on his own. Therefore, you need to keep the bidding going. You must respond, and keep responding, until a game is reached.

Use the same bidding response strategy like responding to 1 in a suit. Respond by bidding your partners suit, a suit of your own or, if you don't have any suit to bid, respond with 2 No Trump. Jump up a level when you have opening hand of 12-15 points. For example, if your partner opens 2 ♥ and you have a strong Diamond hand with 12–15 points, respond with a 4 ♦ bid. This tells your partner your point total and your strongest suit.

## Responding to 3 in a suit:

When your partner opens 3 in a suit, it means he has 6-10 points and at least 7 cards in that suit. He can win 6 to 7 tricks from his hand alone. If you have 10 or fewer points, you should pass. Your partner is hoping that you can win 2 to 3 tricks in your hand which should just allow your partner to make his bid and no more. If you have an opening hand you should raise the bid in his suit.

♠  ♦

## Other Examples of response bids:

### Option 1:

| Opening Bid |
|---|
| 2 ♦ |

**Your hand:**

♠ K 9 7

♥ 10 7 5 2

♣ Q 2

♦ J 10 4 2

7 points
Strong Diamonds
No biddable suit

**Your response**
3 ♦

### Option 2:

| Opening Bid |
|---|
| 3 ♣ |

**Your hand**

♠ A 9 3

♥ K 10 7 3

♣ Q 9 7 2

♦ A 4

14 points
Strong Clubs
Biddable Heart suit

**Your response**
5 ♣

### Option 3:

| Opening Bid |
|---|
| 1 ♠ |

**Your hand**

♠ K Q 9

♥ A 9 5

♣ Q 10 6 2

♦ A 8 7

15 points
Strong Spades
Biddable Club suit

**Your response**
3 ♠

## ~ Quick Tip ~

### Stick to the Points

If football is a game of inches, like they say, Bridge is a game of points. Even the card distribution is converted into points. Your honor and distribution points are the indicators of the strength and weakness of your hand. So, when you bid, always stick to your points.

# The table below shows you the various response bids to suit openings:

## Table 2: Suit Response Bids

| Opening | Response | Comments |
|---------|----------|----------|
| **1 suit** (13-21) | 6-9 points, and no biddable suit: bid 1 No Trump. | When you bid No Trump, count only the honors points, not the distribution points. |
| | 6-9 points & 3 Trumps: respond 2 in the opening suit. 12+ points: jump to the next level forcing a game. | Even if your partner has a low opening of 13 points, if you have 12 points that's 25 total, and enough for a game. |
| | 7-10 points & 4 cards or more in a new suit: respond in the new suit. 12+ points: jump up a level. | Choose a major suit over a minor suit. If you have two equal suits, bid the higher rank first. |
| **2 suit** (21-25) | 0-6 points: bid 2 No Trumps. 7 points plus: bid any Trump. You must keep responding until game is reached. | Opening two is a demand bid. You must not say pass even with 0 points. |
| **3 suit** (6-10) | 7-10 points: pass, 12-15 points: respond 4 or 5 in the opening suit. | Think that your partner can make 6-7 quick tricks. How many can you add from your hand? |

## Responding to "1 No Trump" Opening:

When your partner opens 1 in a suit, it could be minimum hand of 13-15 points, medium hand of 16-18 points or maximum hand of 19-21 points. You really don't know and, unless you have 6 points or more in your hand, you should pass. On the other hand, when your partner opens 1 No Trump, it is easy to figure it out. It always means 15-17 points and even distribution. No guess, no mess.

Even with 0 points in your hand, you shouldn't respond with a pass to 1 NT opening. Playing 1 no trump might not be a good idea especially with your weak hand. The best response with 0-7 points is bidding your longest suit of 5+ cards even if your longest suit has no honors.

If your longest suit is Clubs, you respond 2 ♣. With 10+ points, you jump to 3 ♣.

## Responding to "2 No Trump" Opening:

If your partner opens 2 NT, that means he has 20-21 points and even distribution. With 5-8 points in your hand, you should go to 3 NT.

## Responding to "3 No Trump" Opening:

When your partner opens 3 NT, that is enough for a game using only his hand strength, 25-27 points. If you have 8-12 points, you can go immediately to slam. 8-9 points are enough for 6 NT (small slam), and 12 points are enough for 7 NT (grand slam).

**The table below shows you the various response bids to No Trump opening:**

### Table 3: NT Response Bids

| Opening | Response | Comments |
|---|---|---|
| **1 No Trump** (15-17) | 0-7 points, and long suit of 5+ cards: respond 2 in your long suit even with no honors. 10+ points: jump to 3 No Trump. | Even if you have 0 points you must respond to 1 No Trump with your longest suit. |
| **2 No Trump** (20-21) | 5-8 points: respond 3 No Trump. | Even if your partner has 20 points, your team has enough for a game. |
| **3 No Trump** (25-27) | 7 points: bid 4 No Trump, 8-11 points: bid 6 No Trump, 12 points: bid 7 No Trump. | Just add your points to your partner's points, and it will be easy to bid. 25 points are enough for 3 NT, with 33 points bid 6 NT, and with 37 points bid 7 NT. |

BIDDING

# Examples of responding bids to "No Trump" opening:

| Opening Bid<br>1 NT | Opening Bid<br>2 NT | Opening Bid<br>3 NT |
|---|---|---|
| **Your hand** | **Your hand** | **Your hand** |
| ♠ Q J 5 | ♠ K 9 7 | ♠ K 9 7 |
| ♥ 10 7 | ♥ 10 7 5 2 | ♥ 10 7 5 2 |
| ♣ 9 8 7 | ♣ Q 2 | ♣ Q 10 6 |
| ♦ J 10 8 4 2 | ♦ J 10 4 2 | ♦ A 8 7 |
| 5 points<br>5+ cards in Diamonds<br>Bid your long suit | 6 honor points<br>No biddable suit<br>No void, no singleton | 9 points<br>You can win 3 tricks<br>No void, no singleton |
| **Your response**<br>2 ♦ | **Your response**<br>3 NT | **Your response**<br>6 NT |

♠    ♦

## Overcall Bid:

The overcall bid is the first bid by the opponents after the opening bid. If you open bidding and your opponent made a bid, that's called an *overcall bid*.

In the next table, Table 4: Overcall Bid, you will see most of the overcall options and the overcall responses.

### Table 4: Overcall Bid

| Overcall | Suit | Comments | Response |
|---|---|---|---|
| **1 suit** (10-17 points): overcall at the 1st level. | 5 card suit with 2+ top honors. (Aces, Kings, or Queens) | At the one level, you can overcall with as low as 10 points. | 6-9 points and 3 Trumps: respond 2 in the overcall suit. 12-15 points: jump to the next level not forcing a game. |
| **2 suit** (13-17 points): overcall at the 2nd level. | 5 card suit with 2+ top honors. (Aces, Kings, or Queens) | At the two level, you must have opening points to overcall. | 6-9 points and 3 Trumps: respond 3 in the overcall suit. 12-15 points: go to game. |
| **1 No Trump** (15-17 points) | The opponent's opening suit must be well protected. It means you should have 1 or 2 sure winners in your opponent's opening suit. | You must be prepared to play it, if you have to. Also must have balanced distribution 4-3-3-3, or 4-4-3-2, or 5-3-3-2. | 0-7 points, and long suit of 5+ cards: respond 2 in your long suit even with no honors. 10+ points: jump to the next level. |

♣   ♥

## Table 4: Overcall Bids, continued

| Overcall | Suit | Comments | Response |
|---|---|---|---|
| **3 suit or more** (pre-emptive) | (6-10 points) plus 7+ cards in one suit.<br><br>Usually to stop your opponents from scoring a second game and winning the rubber. | Before you bid, count your quick tricks, and add 2 if vulnerable*, or add 3 when not vulnerable**. Might get a double, and might go down. | 7-10 points: pass. 12-15 points: go to game. |

\* Vulnerable: already won a game.
\*\* Not Vulnerable: have not won a game yet.

## Bidding to Score a Game

It takes 100 points to score a game. You need to score 4 tricks over book (10 tricks) in Spades or Hearts to win a game in a major suit. You need to win 5 tricks over book (11 tricks) in Diamonds or Clubs to win a game in a minor suit. However, you only need 3 tricks over book (9 tricks) in no trumps to win a game in NT.

**The table below shows how many tricks are needed to score a game.**

| Enough Tricks for a Game | Total Score |
|---|---|
| 3 No Trumps (40+30+30) | 100 pts |
| 4 Spades (4x30) | 120 pts |
| 4 Hearts (4x30) | 120 pts |
| 5 Diamonds (5x20) | 100 pts |
| 5 Clubs (5x20) | 100 pts |

You need to score two games in order to win the rubber. The two games don't have to be in sequence. You could win a game and that will be 1 game to 0, then your opponents can win a game, and that will be 1 game to 1. Once you or your opponent wins a second game, the rubber is over, and the winner collects the bonus for the rubber. You can also win the rubber with 2 games to 0.

## Game Points:

According to the most current bridge guidelines, you must have in your hand and your partner's hand a total of 25 points and even distribution to make a 3 No Trump game, or 25 points and total of 8 trump cards to make 4 in a major suit (Spades or Hearts), or 29 points and 8 trump cards to make 5 in a minor suit (Diamonds or Clubs).

| Game | Required Team Points |
|---|---|
| 3 No Trumps (9 tricks) | 25 pts |
| 4 Spades (10 tricks) | 25 pts |
| 4 Hearts (10 tricks) | 25 pts |
| 5 Diamonds (11 tricks) | 29 pts |
| 5 Clubs (11 tricks) | 29 pts |
| 6 small slam (12 tricks) | 33 pts |
| 7 grand slam (13 tricks) | 37 pts |

When you bid in No Trumps, only count your honor points. For all other suits, count both your honor and your distribution points.

If you bid and score 6 in any suit, that's called a *small slam*. You will receive a small slam bonus. If you bid and score 7 tricks in any suit, that's called a *grand slam* and is the highest score in Bridge. You will receive a grand slam bonus.

## ~ *Quick Tip* ~

### Bidding for a Game

When you have enough points for a game, you should always bid for a game. If you don't have enough points to bid a whole game, stop at a *partial game*. Although making a game is more desirable than a partial game, don't get caught in a trap of reaching beyond your points and then finding yourself not making your bid most of the time.

# BRIDGE GAME SUMMARY

♣    ♥

# PLAYING THE HAND

When you are the Declarer and playing the hand, your goal is to win the most tricks possible. You are either playing a trump contract or no trump contract. They are very different. Every trick matters and every card matters. You must keep your focus on playing the hand from the first trick to the last.

## The Opening Lead

Often times the most difficult play in the bridge game is the opening lead. It can be difficult to figure out which card to play and in which suit. The defender on the left of the declarer is the one to do it.

You can summarize the preference in picking the opening lead in the following order:

1.  Play in your partner's strength.
2.  Play in your own strength.
3.  Play in the un-bid suit.
4.  Play in the Dummy's strength.
5.  Play in the trump suit.

♠   ♦                                                   **35**

# BRIDGE GAME SUMMARY

## The best card to lead in a Suit Contract:

### Table 5: Lead Card – Suit Contract

| Condition | Cards | Suit | Lead |
|---|---|---|---|
| If your partner made a bid, lead in your partner's suit. If you have two honors in your partner's suit, play the highest. If you have 1 honor, play the lowest card except if the honor is the Ace. Always play the Ace. | If you have an Ace in your partner's suit. | AXX | Ace |
| | 2 card suit, or 2 card sequence, play the highest. | J10 | J |
| | 3 card sequence, play the highest. | KQJ | K |
| | 3 card suit headed by 2 honors, play the highest. | QJX | Q |
| | 4 card suit headed by 2 honors, play the highest. | KQXX | K |
| | 1 honor in a 3 or 4 card suit, play the lowest. | KXX | X |
| If your partner has not made a bid. The rule still applies. If you have two honors in a suit, play the highest. If you have 1 honor, play the lowest card. In this case you don't always play the Ace. If you have AQX, don't play the Ace. You might win 2 tricks if you wait. | 2 card suit, or 2 card sequence, play the highest. | AK | Ace |
| | 3 card sequence, play the highest. | KQJ | K |
| | 1 honor in a 3 or 4 card suit, play the lowest. | KXX | X |
| | Ace, Queen sequence | AQX | Do not lead this suit |

♣ ♥

## The best card to lead in NT Contract:

### Table 6: Lead Card – NT Contract

| Condition | Cards | Suit | Lead |
|---|---|---|---|
| If your partner has not made a bid. Lead your own suit. If you don't have a suit, lead in the Dummy's bid suit that declarer didn't respond to. | Lead the 4th highest from your longest suit. | QJ9732 | 7 |
| | Lead the lowest from 3 or 4 card suit. | Q105 | 5 |
| | Lead the highest from 2 card suit. | J9 | J |

# Opening The Dummy's Hand:

After the player on the left of the Declarer leads, the Declarer's partner becomes the "Dummy". He opens his cards, puts them on the table face up, and does not participate in playing the hand. The Declarer will play both his hand and his partner's hand.

The Dummy lays the cards down one suit at a time starting with the trump on the left, then the highest opposite color, then he alternates the last two colors. The Declarer should always thank the Dummy for doing that.

If the trump was Spades, then the Dummy lays down his cards as shown in the next figure.

♠  ♦

### Dummy's Hand:

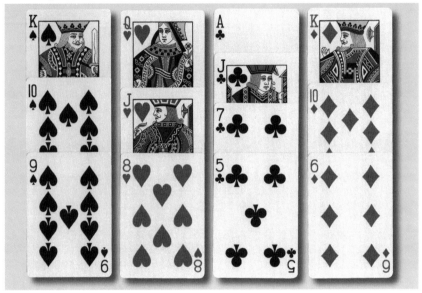

## After the first lead:

Now you are the Declarer and it's your turn to play from the Dummy's hand, so what should you do?

## 1. Count your winning Tricks:

Follow the next exercise to practice counting winning tricks in both your hand and the Dummy's hand combined.

Remember, these examples show the most possible tricks you can make, but good defense by your opponents or bad distribution can make some of these tricks disappear.

| Your Hand | ♠ A X X X |
|---|---|
| | ♥ A X X |
| | ♣ A X X |
| | ♦ A X X |

4 Winning tricks – the 4 Aces

| Your Hand | ♠ A K Q J 10 |
|---|---|
| | ♥ 9 5 3 |
| | ♣ A Q 2 |
| | ♦ K 4 |

8 Winning tricks – the 8 Honors

| Dummy | ♠ A K 9 3 |
|---|---|
| | ♥ Q 10 9 8 |
| | ♣ K 5 |
| | ♦ 10 5 3 |

| Declarer | ♠ 10 9 5 |
|---|---|
| | ♥ |
| | ♣ A Q J 10 8 7 6 2 |
| | ♦ 8 4 |

11 winning tricks when playing in Clubs. 2 in Spades, 1 in Hearts, and 8 in Clubs.

| Dummy | ♠ Q J 5 2 |
|---|---|
| | ♥ K Q 9 8 7 |
| | ♣ |
| | ♦ J 4 3 2 |

| Declarer | ♠ A K 10 9 8 3 |
|---|---|
| | ♥ 5 |
| | ♣ A Q 7 4 |
| | ♦ A 9 |

12 winning tricks when playing in Spades. 6 in Spades, 2 in Hearts, 2 in Clubs and 2 in Diamonds.

| Dummy | ♠ J 10 6 |
|---|---|
| | ♥ K Q 9 5 |
| | ♣ A Q 2 |
| | ♦ Q 9 7 |

| Declarer | ♠ K 9 3 |
|---|---|
| | ♥ A 8 5 |
| | ♣ 6 2 |
| | ♦ A K J 10 4 |

12 winning tricks when playing in Diamonds. 2 in Spades, 3 in Hearts, 2 in Clubs and 5 in Diamonds.

| Dummy | ♠ K J 5 3 |
|---|---|
| | ♥ J 8 4 |
| | ♣ K Q J 7 |
| | ♦ Q 10 |

| Declarer | ♠ A 9 6 |
|---|---|
| | ♥ K 10 9 4 |
| | ♣ A 10 2 |
| | ♦ K 4 3 |

11 winning tricks when playing in NT. 3 in Spades, 2 in Hearts, 4 in Clubs and 2 in Diamonds

## 2. Check for ruffing or crossruffing:

*Ruffing* is trumping that is done on purpose. You play from the Dummy and trump from your hand, or play from your hand and trump from the Dummy. If you can do it both ways at the same time, that's *crossruffing*, and a great way to increase your trump winning tricks.

## 3. Check for an opportunity to establish long suit:

A long suit is a suit where you or your Dummy have a 5-card suit or more, headed by at least two honors. In even distribution, 3 rounds of play in any suit will use 12 cards and leave 1 card left which becomes a "master", (i.e. a definite winner). If you have 5 cards in a suit, your first 4 cards will usually collect the suit and leave you with 1 master. If you have 6 cards, you'll end up with 2 masters.

## 4. Find out if you need to finesse and in which direction:

*Finesse* is a play designed to take away a winner from your opponents. The cards must lie in the right position in order for this to work. Below are two finesse opportunities.

♣   ♥

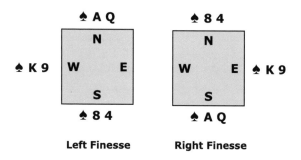

**Left Finesse**          **Right Finesse**

In the left finesse, the cards are set perfectly to finesse the King on the left. You play a low card from your hand and if the King didn't drop, you play the Queen from the Dummy.

In the right finesse, you lead from the Dummy and you finesse the King on your right by playing the Queen if the King wasn't played.

> ## ~ *Quick Tip* ~
> ### Playing the Hand
> When playing a suit contract, collect your trumps first to avoid surprises. Only in special cases would you delay collecting trumps (like in ruffing and crossruffing). When playing a no trump contract, get rid of your losers first so you can cash your winners without interruptions.

♠  ♦                                                    **41**

## 5. Check your entries to your hand and the Dummy:

If you play a card from your hand and the Dummy wins the trick, that's an entry to the Dummy because the next play will be from the Dummy. If you play a card from the Dummy and your hand wins, that's an entry to your hand.

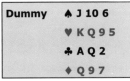

| Dummy | ♠ J 10 6 |
|---|---|
| | ♥ K Q 9 5 |
| | ♣ A Q 2 |
| | ♦ Q 9 7 |

Possible 5 entries

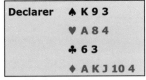

| Declarer | ♠ K 9 3 |
|---|---|
| | ♥ A 8 4 |
| | ♣ 6 3 |
| | ♦ A K J 10 4 |

Possible 6 entries

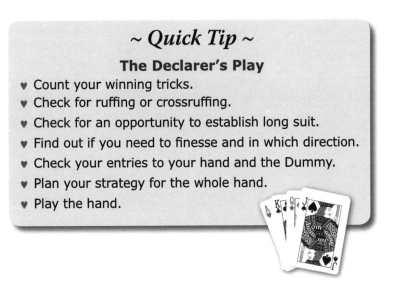

## ~ Quick Tip ~

### The Declarer's Play

- ♥ Count your winning tricks.
- ♥ Check for ruffing or crossruffing.
- ♥ Check for an opportunity to establish long suit.
- ♥ Find out if you need to finesse and in which direction.
- ♥ Check your entries to your hand and the Dummy.
- ♥ Plan your strategy for the whole hand.
- ♥ Play the hand.

♣   ♥

# PLAYING A SLAM

There are two slams in Bridge:

- Small slam – winning 12 tricks

- Grand slam – winning all 13 tricks in the Bridge game.

## Bidding Suit Slam:

Bidding slam in a suit is different than NT. When you bid NT you only count the honor points and not the distribution points, but when you bid in a suit you count everything. This will make it tricky, because 33 or 37 points could be missing crucial honors.

That's why you have to know how many Aces there are in your partner's hand, and sometimes how many Kings, before you go to slam. If your partner doesn't have at least one of the two missing Aces, maybe you should stay at 5 and not go to slam.

There are two conventions you can use to ask for Aces or Kings, the Blackwood Convention and the Gerber Convention.

## The Blackwood Convention:

An opening of 1 ♠ indicates a 13 to 21 point hand. If your partner responds 3 ♠ it shows 12-15 points. If your opening bid of 1 ♠ was on the high side, you are in the slam zone. This is the time to use the Blackwood Convention to ask your partner how many Aces he has and to later ask the same question about his Kings, if need be.

**Ask for Aces by jumping to 4 NT:**
**Your partner will respond as follows:**

No Aces:      5 ♣
One Ace:      5 ♦
Two Aces:     5 ♥
Three Aces:   5 ♠
Four Aces:    5 ♣

In spite of the fact that 5 ♣ has two meanings, either no Aces or all Aces, it is easy to distinguish the difference. The 5 ♣ response in almost all cases means no Aces. If you ask for Aces while having none, 5 ♣ will definitely mean 4 Aces.

**Ask for Kings by bidding 5 NT:**
**Your partner will respond as follows:**

No Kings:      6 ♣
One King:      6 ♦
Two Kings:     6 ♥
Three Kings:  6 ♠
Four Kings:    6 ♣

Just like the Aces, you can always tell if your partner's 6 ♣ mean no Kings or 4 Kings, based on how many you have.

## The Gerber Convention:

One drawback to the Blackwood Convention is that your response starts at level five immediately. If your partner doesn't have what you hoped, you don't have much room to maneuver to find your best bid. That's why some players prefer to use the Gerber Convention which also asks for Aces and Kings, but the response starts at level four instead of five.

Using the previous example, if you opened 1 ♠ and your partner responded with 3 ♠. You need to count up your combined points to see if you are in the slam zone. If you decide to try and go for slam, using the Gerber Convention you would then bid 4 ♣.

**Ask for Aces by jumping to 4 Clubs:**
**Your partner will respond as follows:**

No Aces:      4 ♦
One Ace:      4 ♥
Two Aces:     4 ♠
Three Aces:  4 NT
Four Aces:    4 ♦

**Ask for Kings by bidding 5 Clubs:**
**Your partner will respond as follows:**

No Kings:      5 ♦
One King:      5 ♥
Two Kings:     5 ♠
Three Kings: 5 NT
Four Kings:   5 ♦

Before using the Blackwood or Gerber Convention you and your partner need to discuss and agree on using either or both conventions before you start that evening's play. Your opponents need to be aware of that choice as well.

## ~ *Quick Tip* ~

### Bidding for a Slam

You can use the Blackwood Convention to ask your partner for his Aces and Kings by jumping to 4 NT, or use the Gerber Convention by jumping to 4 ♣. These conventions are very important when playing a slam in a suit. If you are playing a slam in NT there is no need to ask your partner for his Aces or Kings. You can rely solely on the point count.

♣    ♥

## Table 7: Slam Summary Table

| Slam | Requirement |
|---|---|
| **Small Slam** bid 6 (12 tricks) | 33 Points |
| **Grand Slam** bid 7 (13 tricks) | 37 Points |
| **NT Slam** | No need to ask for Aces/Kings. |
| **Suit Slam** | Use Blackwood or Gerber convention to ask for Aces/Kings. |
| **The Blackwood Convention** | **Response** |
| **4 NT** Ask for Aces | 5 ♣ : No Aces<br>5 ♦ : One Ace<br>5 ♥ : Two Aces<br>5 ♠ : Three Aces<br>5 ♣ : Four Aces |
| **5 NT** Ask for Kings | 6 ♣ : No Kings<br>6 ♦ : One King<br>6 ♥ : Two Kings<br>6 ♠ : Three Kings<br>6 ♣ : Four Kings |
| **The Gerber Convention** | **Response** |
| **4 Clubs** Ask for Aces | 4 ♦ : No Aces<br>4 ♥ : One Ace<br>4 ♠ : Two Aces<br>4 NT: Three Aces<br>4 ♦ : Four Aces |
| **5 Clubs** Ask for Kings | 5 ♦ : No Kings<br>5 ♥ : One King<br>5 ♠ : Two Kings<br>5 NT: Three Kings<br>5 ♦ : Four Kings |

| Bonus Points | Not Vulnerable | Vulnerable |
|---|---|---|
| Small slam | 500 | 750 |
| Grand slam | 1000 | 1500 |

♠    ♦

# BRIDGE GAME SUMMARY

♣ ♥

# BRIDGE CONVENTIONS

Playing Bridge without using conventions is called "Natural Bridge". You can play Natural Bridge exclusively and enjoy the game without using any Bridge conventions. One exception would be in slam bidding – you need to use a convention to ask your partner for his Aces or Kings.

Over the years, many conventions were developed to help partners know more about each other's hands and increase their chances of winning. Some of those conventions are very simple and some are very complicated. You do not need to use all the conventions when you play Bridge. Just pick the ones that you like, get yourself familiar with them and start using them.

Before the game starts, the players should disclose what conventions they are going to use and explain them to the other players. Everyone should know what every bid means before playing the game. Some conventions are intuitive and always have been part of Natural Bridge before they were classified as conventions. Many times we use Bridge conventions without knowing it. For example, the "Balancing Bid" convention has you bidding with fewer points than usual in order to prevent the opponents from winning a 1 suit bid.

Like winning the hand with just 1 ♠. Bridge players always did that, but just didn't know it was called the Balancing Bid convention.

Another convention that was always used intuitively is "Reverses". Usually you bid your higher ranking suit first, but if your lower ranking suit is longer and stronger, you reverse that and open with the lower ranking suit first. In the second round you bid the other one. We did not think of this as a convention, it was just the right thing to do.

Doubling your opponent bid or doubling your opponent overcall bid are bids we always used while playing Natural Bridge to show our partner that we have opening points but no 5-card suit. Those two situations are also conventions and are called "Takeout Doubles" and "Negative Doubles" respectively.

Another intuitive convention is the "Lead Directing Double". Without the fancy name, it's basically doubling your opponent slam bid. Naturally you never double a slam unless you have a surprise winner, like a void in a suit. So, if you double a slam, your partner will try to figure out in which suit you are most likely void so that he can lead in that suit. That's what the "Lead Directing Double" means.

In addition to those easy, intuitive conventions that were part of our play and we did not think of as organized conventions, there are really smart ones that will impress you. Some of the Bridge conventions are simple like "Stayman","Landy", and

♣ ♥

"Jacoby Transfer". Some need careful study and memorization like "Michaels Cuebid", "Roman Key Card Blackwood", and "Ogust Rebids".

Listed in the tables that follow are brief summaries of the most popular conventions. This is merely a quick reference for Bridge players. If you want to study the conventions in depth, I recommend a great book called *25 Bridge Conventions You Should Know* by Barbara Seagram & Marc Smith, which provides a great detailed resource for Bridge conventions.

## ~ *Quick Tips* ~

### Conventions Disclosure

Before the game starts, the players should disclose the conventions they are going to use and explain them to the other players. Everyone should know what conventions will be used and what every bid means before playing the game.

# BRIDGE GAME SUMMARY

*Note: In the tables following, "Opp." means "Opponent".*

| Name | Description | Reason | Response |
|------|-------------|--------|----------|
| **Reverses** | Usually, if you have two suits, you open the higher ranking one first. In reverses, you reverse that by opening the lower ranking suit first. Then the 2nd round, You bid your 2nd suit.<br><br>**Opener    Partner**<br>1 ♣        1 ♠<br>2 ♦<br>(Reverse bid) | It tells partner that you have minimum 16 points and your 1st bid suit was longer than the 2nd. Maybe 5-card long and your 2nd 4-card long. | Rebid your own suit, or bid in your partner's 1st or 2nd suit. Or, bid NT.<br><br>**Partner**<br>2 ♠<br>or<br>3 ♣<br>or<br>3 ♦<br>or<br>2 NT |
| **Balancing** | Bidding after two passes to a low level bid.<br><br>**Pass**<br><br>     N<br>1 ♠   W   E   Pass<br>     S<br><br>2 ♥<br>(Balancing Bid) | You can make a balancing bid with less points than a normal direct bid. It will keep the bidding alive for your partner to get a 2nd chance to bid. It will also prevent your opponents from making a cheap hand. | Stay low because you can't go to game in this situation. Most likely all the points are divided equally between the two teams and the most any team can do is a partial game. |
| **Jacoby 2 NT forcing** | 2 NT response to major suit opening (1 ♥ or 1 ♠).<br><br>**Opener    Partner**<br>1 ♠        2 NT | Forcing without going to the 3rd level by bidding 3 ♥ or 3 ♠. | Rebid 3 in your opening suit if you have strong trump support. If not, bid 3 NT. |

♣   ♥

| Name | Description | Reason | Response |
|------|-------------|--------|----------|
| **Short Club Opening** | An artificial bid that doesn't mean you have Clubs. It means you have a solid opening of 13-19 points and no 5-card major suit.<br><br>**Opener**    **Partner**<br>1 ♣      1 ♥<br>        (or 1 ♠) | It asks your partner to bid his 4-card major suit.<br>1 ♥ or 1 ♠. | 7-10 points and 4-card major suit, responds 1 in the major suit. 12-15 points, jump to the next level. |
| **Weak Two Bid** | Weak Two Bid is opening 2 ♦, or 2 ♥, or 2 ♠ with 6-8 points and 6-card suit or longer. It cannot be 2 ♣ because it's reserved for strong opening.<br><br>**Opener**<br>2 ♦<br>or<br>2 ♥<br>or<br>2 ♠ | Low level preemptive bid that confuse bidding for the opponents and tell your partner about your hand. | With no support in the bid suit, partner can pass. Or, response with normal overcall responses. |
| **Two Clubs Strong Opening** | If you use the "Weak Two Bid" convention, then you must use the "Two Clubs Strong Opening" convention when you have a traditional 2 opening hand.<br><br>**Opener**<br>2 ♣ | Shows 22+ points and invites partner to keep bidding until a game is reached. | Partner can not say pass, and may response 2 ♦ if he doesn't have a biddable suit or response in his strong suit (2 ♥, 2 ♠, or 3 ♣). |

| Name | Description | Reason | Response |
|---|---|---|---|
| **Ogust rebids** | When you open with a weak 2 bid and partner responses with 2 NT, you can reply with Ogust rebids.<br><br>**Opener**    **Partner**<br>2 ♦          2 NT<br>3 any suit<br>(Ogust rebid) | To tell your partner more about your weak 2 bid:<br><br>3 ♣:  Min. points, weak suit.<br>3 ♦:  Max. points, good suit.<br>3 ♥:  Max. points, weak suit.<br>3 ♠:  Max. points, good suit.<br>3 NT: Solid suit. | Use natural Bridge to bid in your partner's suit, or in NT or in your own strong suit. |
| **Drury** | A "Drury" is a 2 ♣ response to partner's 3rd or 4th seat opening of 1 ♠ or 1 ♥.<br><br>**Opener**    **Partner**<br>1 ♠          2 ♣<br>or 1 ♥   (Drury)<br>(after 2 or 3 passes) | To signal to your partner that you have a good hand of 10+ points and 3-4 trump cards, while keeping the bidding low in case partner opened with a low hand. | It's now up to the opener to come back with 2 in the opening suit to play partial game, or 4 to play a game. |
| **Fourth suit forcing** | An artificial bid in the forth suit after you and your partner bid the other three suits. In this case your opponents are passing every time.<br><br>**Opener**    **Partner**<br>1 ♥          1 ♠<br>2 ♣         2 ♦<br>             (forcing) | Fourth suit forcing simply tells your partner that we should keep bidding until a game is reached. | Reply by bidding for a game. |

| Name | Description | Reason | Response |
|------|-------------|--------|----------|
| **New minor forcing** | In the second round of bidding, replying to partner's 1 NT in a new minor suit is forcing.<br><br>**Opener    Partner**<br>1 ♣        1 ♥<br>1 NT      2 ♦<br>              (forcing) | New minor forcing, is a way to ask your partner to explore going for a game. | Use natural Bridge to find the right fit and to decide if you can go to a game. |
| **Help suit Game Tries** | When opener 2nd bid is in the suit that needs partner's help. Usually the suit with two or more losers.<br><br>**Opener    Partner**<br>1 ♠        2 ♠<br>3 ♥        3 ♠ (no help)<br>(asking    4 ♠ (got help)<br>for help<br>in ♥) | If partner can help with the opener weak suit, then game is achievable even with less points. | Bid in the opener weak suit if you have 4-card headed by 2 honors or bid a game in the opener strong suit. Bid 3 in the opener strong suit if you have no help. |
| **Control showing cuebids** | After a trump is agreed upon, your cuebid is a bid in your lowest suit where you have the 1st round of control.<br><br>**Opener    Partner**<br>1 ♣        1 ♠<br>3 ♠        4 ♣, 4 ♦, 4 ♥<br>              (Any of of those bids are cuebids) | It shows the suit where you have an Ace or void that will win the 1st round of play. | Partner will do the same by cuebidding his lowest suit with 1st round of control. |

♠    ♦

| Name | Description | Reason | Response |
|------|-------------|--------|----------|
| **Splinter Bid** | Double jump in response to 1 major suit opening. It helps going to slam with fewer points.<br><br>**Opener   Partner**<br>1 ♠         4 ♣, 4 ♦, 4 ♥<br>                (Splinter Bid) | To show an opening hand and to bid your void or singleton suit at the same time. When you reply 4 ♣ to 1 ♠ opening, you're forcing and saying that you have void or singleton in Clubs. | Stop at a game or go to slam based on distributions and cards fit. |
| **Cuebid Raises** | Cuebid is bidding in a suit that is not going to be your team's trump suit, like bidding in your opponent suit.<br><br>**Opener**<br>1 ♠<br><br>N<br>W    E    2 ♣<br>S<br><br>3 ♣<br>(Cuebid Raise) | It's one more bid choice you can use to show your partner that you have 3 cards in his bid suit, and 6-9 points. If your hand is stronger or you have more trump cards, you shouldn't use Cuebid and bid naturally. | It will be up to your partner to go to a game or stay low. |
| **Stayman** | 2 ♣ response to 1 NT<br><br>**Opener   Partner**<br>1 NT        2 ♣<br>                (Stayman) | Asking partner to bid a 4-card major suit. | 2 ♥ : 4-card ♥ suit,<br>2 ♠ : 4-card ♠ suit,<br>2 ♦ : no 4-card major suit. |

♣   ♥

| Name | Description | Reason | Response |
|------|-------------|--------|----------|
| Jacoby Transfers | A response to partner's 1 NT opening by bidding 2 in the suit before your intended suit. Thus transferring the bidding in your intended suit to your partner.<br><br>**Opener** **Partner**<br>1 NT 2 ♥<br>2 ♠ (Spade<br>(Bid spade Transfer)<br>to complete the transfer) | To make sure that the partner who has the strong hand becomes the declarer. | Must response in the intended suit to complete the transfer. If partner bids 2 ♦, you bid 2 ♥. If he bids 2 ♥, you bid 2 ♠. |
| Lebensohl | When your partner opens 1 NT and your opponent overcalls 2 in any suit. Lebensohl is a 2 NT reply to your partner.<br><br>**Opener**<br>1 NT<br><br>N W E S 2 (Any Suit)<br><br>**Partner**<br>2 NT<br>(Lebensohl) | It tells your partner that you have a stopper (a winner) in your opponent suit and forces your partner to reply 3 Clubs to send the bidding back to you. | Now you can bid 3 NT, or inquire about your partner's 4-cards suit by bidding 3 in your opponent's suit, or bid 3 in your own strong suit. |

| Name | Description | Reason | Response |
|---|---|---|---|
| **Takeout Doubles** | "Double" response to opponent's 1 suit opening.<br><br>**Opp.**<br>**Opens**    **You**<br>1 suit     Double<br>           (Takeout Double) | You have opening points but no 5-card suit to open with. It's a call to your partner to name his best unbid suit. Preferably a major suit, and better stay at low level. | Partner must bid his favorite unbid suit even with a weak hand to take out his partner from the double situation. |
| **Negative Doubles** | Doubling an overcall bid.<br><br>**Opener**<br>1 ♦<br><br>**N**<br>**W E**   1 ♣<br>**S**<br><br>**Double**<br>(Negative Double) | Not intended to challenge the opponent bid but to tell your partner that you have points and no biddable (5-card) suit. | Bid one of the unbid suits. |
| **Michaels Cuebid** | An overcall bid that shows two suits at the same time by bidding in the opponent's opening suit.<br><br>**Opp.**<br>**Opens**    **You**<br>1 ♣       2 ♣<br>or          or<br>1 ♦       2 ♦<br>or          or<br>1 ♥       2 ♥<br>or          or<br>1 ♠       2 ♠<br>          (Michaels Cuebids) | If your opponent opens 1 ♣ or 1 ♦, you overcall 2 ♣ or 2 ♦ and that will mean you have Hearts and Spades (the other two major suits). If your opponent opens in a major suit like 1 ♥, then you overcall 2 ♥ meaning you have the other major suit (Spade), plus one minor. If your opponent opens 1 ♠, you overcall 2 ♠ which means you have the other major suit (Hearts), plus one minor suit. | Natural reply to overcall bid by bidding in the major suit with the most fit. Otherwise, refer to the unusual no trump bid below. |

       ♣    ♥

| Name | Description | Reason | Response |
|---|---|---|---|
| Unusual no trump | A 2 NT bid after your partner uses Michaels cuebid.<br><br>2 ♣<br>(Michaels Cuebid)<br><br>1 ♣   N<br>Open   W   E   Pass<br>  S<br>2 NT<br>(Unusual NT) | It tells your partner that you're not interested in his major suit and you'd rather play in his minor suit. | Partner should reply by bidding in his minor suit. |
| Landy | 2 ♣ overcall over opponent's 1 NT opening.<br><br>**Opp.**    **You**<br>**Opens**   2 ♣<br>1 NT     (Landy) | It tells partner that you have both major suits similar to the meaning of Michael's cuebid 2 Clubs response. | With a fit in one of the two major suits and 10-12 points, reply 3 in your major suit. |
| Responsive doubles | Your opponent opened the bidding with 1 in a suit. Your partner doubled (or bid a suit without raising). Your other opponent replied 2 in his partner's open-ing suit. It's your turn to bid. If your bid is double, this is a "Re-sponsive double".<br><br>**Partner**<br>Double<br>(or suit bid)<br><br>1 ♣   N<br>Open   W   E   2 ♣<br>  S<br>**You**<br>Double<br>(Responsive Double) | It tells your partner that you have at least 2 out of the 3 unbid suits. Or, you have the 2 unbid suits and some help in your partner's suit. | Reply in your best suit, you might find a good fit and take the hand away from your opponents. |

♠   ♦

| Name | Description | Reason | Response |
|---|---|---|---|
| **Blackwood Convention**<br><br>**Gerber Convention** | See "Playing a Slam" section | | |
| **Grand slam force** | Bidding 5 NT (after a trump suit is agreed upon) to ask your partner if he has 2 of the top 3 trump honors.<br><br>**Opener   Partner**<br>2 ♠         5 NT | To make sure that your team has all top trump honors before bidding for a grand slam. | Bid 7 if you have 2 of the top 3 honors in the agreed trump suit. Bid 6 if you don't. |
| **Roman Key Card Blackwood** | A response to the normal 4 NT Blackwood bid that tells partner if you have the king of trump in addition to your aces. RKC Blackwood considers the 4 aces and the king of trump as the 5 key cards.<br><br>**You: 4 NT**<br><br>**Partner:**<br>5 ♣ : 1 or 4 key cards.<br>5 ♦ : 3 or 0 key cards<br>5 ♥ : 2 or 5 key cards (no Queen of trump).<br>5 ♠ : 2 or 5 Key cards (with the Queen of trump) | Knowing if your partner has the king and/or the queen of trump is sometimes essential in slam bidding. | Based on your partner's response, go to Slam or stay at 5. |

♣   ♥

| Name | Description | Reason | Response |
|---|---|---|---|
| Lead-Directing Doubles | Lead directing double is doubling a slam bid in order to tell your partner to make an unusual lead.<br><br>**Opponent**   **You**<br>6 ♠          Double | It tells your partner that you have a void and he shouldn't lead the usual way. Partner should make an unusual lead in the suit you most likely have your void. | Partner should lead in the Dummy's suit or the declarer side suit, or figure out which suit is the most likely suit for you to be void. |

## ~ *Quick Tips* ~

### Bridge Etiquette

The ACBL (American Contract Bridge League) states that a player should refrain from:

- ♥ Paying insufficient attention.
- ♥ Making gratuitous comments during the play as to the auction or the adequacy of the contract.
- ♥ Detaching a card from the hand before it is that player's turn.
- ♥ Arranging the cards played to previous tricks in a disorderly manner or mixing the cards together before the result has been agreed to.
- ♥ Making a questionable claim or concession.
- ♥ Prolonging the play unnecessarily.

# BRIDGE GAME SUMMARY

♣   ♥

# KEEPING THE SCORE

## Summary:

1. Everyone should know how to keep the score in Bridge. Knowing how the scoring system works is crucial to the bidding process.

2. The score pad is divided into two columns, one for each team. "We" indicates the team that is keeping the score, and "They" being the other team. The score pad also has a horizontal line dividing the pad into an upper section and lower section. Some of the score is written over that dividing line and some written under the line.

3. When you make your bid, you receive points for your contracted tricks under the line. That could be for a full game or partial game. If you get overtricks they will be scored above the line.

4. The Declarer get penalized for not fulfilling his contract. The penalty points go to the opponents and are written above the line.

5. When you receive any bonuses for the rubber, for a slam, for having 4 honors in one suit, etc... all bonuses are written above the line.

6. The winner is the one with the most points including all points above and below the line.

You can see below an example of a bridge score pad.

| We | They |
|---|---|
| **All other points** | |
| **Game points** | |

**Score Card**

## ~ *Quick Tip* ~

### Scoring Games and Rubbers

A game is a score of 100 points or more either by bidding and playing one hand to score a whole game, or by bidding and playing partial games. The Rubber is a set of two games won by one team. In the score pad, use a separate page for each Rubber and add up all the points at the end of the page including Rubber bonus points.

## Example of Scoring a Simple (2 games to 1) rubber

| We | They |
|----|------|
|  |  |
|  |  |
| 30 |  |
| 120 |  |
|  |  |
|  |  |

### After 1st hand:

**We:** Bid 4 Hearts, but made 5 Hearts. Write game points (4 x 30 =120) under the line, and points for extra tricks (1 x 30=30) above the line.

| We | They |
|----|------|
|  |  |
|  |  |
| 30 |  |
| 120 |  |
| 60 |  |
|  |  |
|  |  |

### After 2nd hand:

**We:** Bid 2 Spades, and made it. Write partial game points (2 x 30 = 60) under the line. Now "**We**" have "a leg" in the game equal to 60 points.

*Note: A line across the pad was drawn under the "120" to separate the first game from the next.*

| We | They |
|----|------|
|    |      |
| 30 |      |
| 120 |     |
| 60 | 40   |

### After 3rd hand:

**They:** Bid 2 Clubs, and made it. Write partial game points (2 x 20 = 40) under the line. Now "**They**" also have "a leg" in the game equal to 40 points.

| We | They |
|----|------|
|    |      |
| 30 |      |
| 120 |     |
| 60 | 40   |
|    | 60   |

### After 4th hand:

**They:** Bid 2 Hearts, and made it. Write the score (2 x 30 = 60) under the line. "**They**" have a game now. Draw a line across the pad. The 60 point leg that "**We**" had is now cut off, and will no longer count toward partial game points. However, the points still counts toward your overall score.

♣  ♥

### After 5th hand:

**We:** Bid 5 Clubs, and made it. Write game points (5 x 20 =100) under the line. Now the rubber is over. Write 500 bonus points for winning the rubber (2 games to 1), above the line. (Bonus points for winning the rubber 2 games to 0 is 700 points). Total the points, 810 for **We**, and 100 for **They**.

**We:** won by 710 points. Approx. 700 points.

If you change partners every rubber, and want to know the winner at the end of the game, you divide the points by 100, so you give each player in "**We**" +7 points, and each player in "**They**" -7 points. You do the same every rubber and at the end of the match add up the score for each player and find out the winner.

| | We | They |
|---|---|---|
| | | |
| | 500 | |
| | 30 | |
| | 120 | |
| | 60 | 40 |
| | | 60 |
| | 100 | |
| | | |
| **Total** | 810 | 100 |

## Doubles, Downs, and Bonus Points:

- Any team can challenge the bid of the other team by saying "Double", and sometimes they get a "Re-double" in return. Double means if you make your bid your points will be doubled. If you lose your bid, for every trick you go down, your opponents will gain two times or more the points they would normally get. If you say re-double after your opponents have doubled your bid, it will mean that you will gain or lose even more points depending on the outcome of the hand.

- When you have won a game you are "Vulnerable". Now the points your opponents receive when you do not make your bid are higher. Also, any overtricks you make will be worth more and your slam bonuses will give you more points.

You can refer to the tables on the next few pages for penalties and bonuses when doubled or re-doubled, and for vulnerable or not vulnerable.

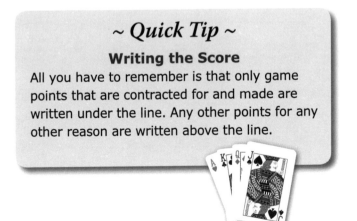

*~ Quick Tip ~*

**Writing the Score**

All you have to remember is that only game points that are contracted for and made are written under the line. Any other points for any other reason are written above the line.

## Table 8: Downs Value*

| Downs | Not Vulnerable | | | Vulnerable | | |
|-------|---------------|---------|-----------|-----------|---------|-----------|
| | Un-doubled | Doubled | Re-Doubled | Un-doubled | Doubled | Re-Doubled |
| 1 | 50 | 100 | 200 | 100 | 200 | 400 |
| 2 | 100 | 300 | 600 | 200 | 500 | 1000 |
| 3 | 150 | 500 | 1000 | 300 | 800 | 1600 |
| 4 | 200 | 800 | 1600 | 400 | 1100 | 2200 |
| 5 | 250 | 1100 | 2200 | 500 | 1400 | 2800 |
| 6 | 300 | 1400 | 2800 | 600 | 1700 | 3400 |
| 7 | 350 | 1700 | 3400 | 700 | 2000 | 4000 |
| 8 | 400 | 2000 | 4000 | 800 | 2300 | 4600 |
| 9 | 450 | 2300 | 4600 | 900 | 2600 | 5200 |
| 10 | 500 | 2600 | 5200 | 1000 | 2900 | 5800 |
| 11 | 550 | 2900 | 5800 | 1100 | 3200 | 6400 |
| 12 | 600 | 3200 | 6400 | 1200 | 3500 | 7000 |
| 13 | 650 | 3500 | 7000 | 1300 | 3800 | 7600 |

## Table 9: Tricks Value

| Tricks | Not Vulnerable | | | Vulnerable | | |
|--------|---------------|---------|-----------|-----------|---------|-----------|
| | Un-doubled | Doubled | Re-Doubled | Un-doubled | Doubled | Re-Doubled |
| Club | 20 | 40 | 80 | 20 | 40 | 80 |
| Diamond | 20 | 40 | 80 | 20 | 40 | 80 |
| Heart | 30 | 60 | 120 | 30 | 60 | 120 |
| Spade | 30 | 60 | 120 | 30 | 60 | 120 |
| 1st No Trump | 40 | 80 | 160 | 40 | 80 | 160 |
| No Trump | 30 | 60 | 120 | 30 | 60 | 120 |
| Over Tricks | Trick value | 100 | 200 | Trick value | 200 | 400 |
| Bonus for making a doubled contract: 50 | | | | | | |

* Downs are the losing tricks below the contracted bid.

69

## Table 10: Bonus Points

| Plays | Bonus |
|---|:---:|
| Rubber 2-0 game | 700 |
| Rubber 2-1 game | 500 |
| Unfinished rubber (1 game) | 300 |
| Partial game score | 50 |
| 4 honors, A K Q J in one suit* | 100 |
| 5 honors, A K Q J 10 in one suit* | 150 |
| 4 Aces when playing No Trump | 150 |

\* When playing that suit

## Table 11: Slam Bonus

| Slam – Bid and Made | Not Vulnerable | Vulnerable |
|---|:---:|:---:|
| Small slam (12 tricks) | 500 | 750 |
| Grand slam (13 tricks) | 1000 | 1500 |

### ~ Quick Tip ~

#### Slam Bonus

You receive 500 bonus points for scoring a small slam, and 1000 for a grand slam. If you are vulnerable you receive 750 points for a small slam and 1500 points for a grand slam. Making 12 or 13 tricks without bidding for a slam is not considered a slam and doesn't receive bonus points.

# Glossary

**Balancing:** Bidding after two passes to a low level opening bid.

**Blackwood Convention:** An artificial bid used in slam bidding and starts at the 4 No Trumps level. It's used to ask your partner for the number of Aces and the number of Kings in his hand.

**Book:** The 1st 6 tricks won by the Declarer.

**Contract:** A promise to win a specific number of tricks.

**Control showing cuebids:** After a trump is agreed upon, control showing cuebid is a bid in your lowest suit where you have the 1st round of control.

**Cuebid Raises:** Cuebid Raises is bidding in a suit that is not going to be your team's trump suit, like bidding in your opponent suit.

**Dealer:** The player whose turn it is to deal the cards.

**Declarer:** The winner of the bidding and the one that will play the hand.

**Doubleton:** Holding two cards of any suit.

**Drury:** A "Drury" is a 2 ♣ response to partner's 3rd or 4th seat opening of 1 ♠ or 1 ♥.

**Dummy:** The declarer's partner that lays down his cards.

**Finesse:** Turning your opponent's winning card into a loser.

**Fourth suit forcing:** An artificial bid in the fourth suit after you and your partner bid the other three suits. In this case your opponents are passing every time.

**Game:** Bidding and making 100 points or more.

**Gerber Convention:** An artificial bid used in slam bidding and starts at the 4 Clubs level. It's used to ask your partner for the number of Aces and the number of Kings in his hand.

**Grand slam:** Bidding and winning 7 in a suit or 7 in No Trump. That's 13 tricks which is all the tricks in the hand.

**Grand slam force:** Bidding 5 NT ( after a trump suit is agreed upon) to ask your partner if he has 2 of the top 3 trump honors.

**Hand:** The hand is the playing of the cards after they are dealt.

**Help suit Game Tries:** When opener 2nd bid is in the suit that needs partner's help. Usually the suit with two or more losers.

**Honors:** The 4 honors in every suit are the Ace, King, Queen, and the Jack. Sometimes the 10 is called the 5th honor.

**Jacoby 2 NT forcing:** 2 NT response to major suit opening (1 ♥ or 1 ♠).

**Jacoby Transfers:** A response to partner's 1 NT opening by bidding 2 in the suit before your intended suit. Thus transferring the bidding in your intended suit to your partner.

**Jump:** Bid higher than the immediate next level.

**Landy: 2 ♣ over opponents' 1 NT:** 2 ♣ overcall over opponent's 1 NT opening.

**Lead directing doubles:** Lead directing double is doubling a slam bid in order to tell your partner to make an unusual lead.

**Lebensohl:** When your partner opens 1 NT and your opponent overcalls 2 in any suit. Lebensohl is a 2 NT reply to your partner.

♣   ♥

**Long suit:** 6 cards or longer

**Major suit:** Spades or Hearts.

**Michaels cuebid:** An overcall bid that shows two suits at the same time by bidding in the opponent's opening suit.

**Minor suit:** Clubs or Diamonds.

**Negative Doubles:** Doubling an overcall bid.

**New minor forcing:** In the second round of bidding, replying to partner's 1 NT in a new minor suit is forcing.

**No Trump:** Playing without a designated trump suit.

**Not Vulnerable:** The team that has not won a game yet is called "not vulnerable".

**Ogust rebids:** When you open with a weak 2 bid and partner responses with 2 NT, you can reply with Ogust rebids.

**Opening bid:** The 1st bid.

**Opening lead:** The 1st card led before the Dummy lays down his cards.

**Opening points:** 13 or more points.

**Overtrick:** Winning an extra trick over the contracted number of tricks.

**Preemptive bid:** A high opening bid designed to discourage the opponents from bidding.

**Protected suit:** A suit where you have one or more winners.

**Responsive doubles:** Your opponent opened the bidding with 1 in a suit. Your partner doubled (or bid a suit without raising). Your other opponent replied 2 in his partner's opening suit. It's your turn to bid. If your bid is double, this is a "Responsive double".

**Reverses:** Usualy, if you have two suits, you open the higher ranking one first. In reverses, you reverse that by opening the lower ranking suit first.

**Roman key card Blackwood:** A response to the normal 4 NT Blackwood bid that tells partner if you have the king of trump in addition to your aces.

**Round:** When every player has played a card.

**Rubber:** A set of two games won by one team.

**Short Club Opening:** An artifical bid that doesn't mean you have Clubs. It means you have solid openning of 13-19 points and no 5-card major suit. It is designed to ask your partner for his major suit of 4 cards or more.

**Singleton:** Holding one card of any suit.

**Small slam:** Bidding and winning 6 in a suit or 6 in No Trump. That is 12 tricks which is all the tricks in the hand except one.

**Splinter Bid:** Double jump in response to 1 major suit opening. It helps going to slam with fewer points.

**Stayman:** An artificial bid in response to I No Trump. You bid 2 ♣ to ask your partner for his best 4-card major suit.

**Stoppers:** Sure winners in the opponents bid suit.

♣ ♥

**Takeout Doubles:** "Double" response to opponent's 1 suit opening.

**Trick:** A round of play where each player played a card.

**Trick winner:** The player that won the trick using a high card or Trump.

**Trump:** The suit bid for the contract.

**Two Clubs Strong Opening:** If you use the "Weak Two Bid" convention, then you must use the "Two Clubs Strong Opening" convention when you have a traditional 2 opening hand.

**Unusual no trump:** A 2 NT bid after your partner uses Michaels cuebid.

**Void:** Holding no cards in any particular suit.

**Vulnerable:** The team that won their first game is called "vulnerable".

**Weak Two Bid:** Weak Two Bid is opening 2 ♦, or 2 ♥, or 2 ♠ with 6-8 points and 6-card suit or longer. It cannot be 2 ♣ because it's reserved for strong opening.

**Winners:** Cards that will win the trick.

♠   ♦

# About the Author

Samir Riad was born in Cairo, Egypt and earned his bachelors degree in Electrical Engineering from the HIT High Institute of Technology in Helwan, Egypt. His passion for math and physics was only surpassed by his passion for playing Bridge. He would very often stay up all night playing Bridge with his friends. Over the years, he taught many friends how to play the game and was often amazed at how quickly their intimidation diminished and how enthusiastic they became. It was because of this that Samir felt so driven to write this book. His unique teaching method is simple and he hopes it will bring many more people into the incredibly enjoyable world of Bridge playing.

Samir moved to California in 1985 and became a U.S. citizen. He owns a chain of wireless phone stores in the San Francisco Bay Area and currently lives with his wife and children in San Jose, California.

♣    ♥